LEARNING BY LIVING:

LEARNING BY LIVING:

A COLLECTION OF POEMS

ZAFIRA HUDANI

ISBN: Paperback - 979-8-9858418-0-0 / Ebook - 979-8-9858418-1-7
Library of Congress Control Number: 2022908899

Dedicated To:

I want to dedicate this book to *my family*:
My mom, sisters, and my dad.

Thank you for supporting and loving me throughout
my journey.

I would like to note that I am using **poetic license**
in order to express my thoughts and feelings in a
unique and *meaningful* way.

Table of Contents

GOD/PRAYER/SOUL/ SPIRIT/ UNIVERSE

HOLIDAYS

LESSONS

NATURE

Rain

Water from the sky
It is a gift from above
Water is a life source regardless of its source
Protect it and use it wisely
For that is what you will always need

Looking at the Sky

The sky is a beautiful thing
Do you look up at it?
Or are you waiting for your phone to ring?
Do you understand how grand it is to see the sky?
Or are you too busy to even try?
Take some time to look at the sky
Don't let the small things in life pass you by

Different Seasons

There are four seasons in a year
Each with its own challenges
The seasons bring change
Some bring snow, others bring rain

Each season offers a new reason
To see the magic that change can bring
For example, from Winter to Spring
From animals hibernating
To new plants growing in the spring

A tree

Sometimes I think
What a wonder
It stands through lighting and thunder
Some provide lumber
Others provide the air we breath
Which is something we all need
It is the thing that gives us life

If one is taken, two should be planted in its place
This will allow us to show Mother Nature
Our appreciation for allowing trees to grow.

A rainbow

A rainbow comes after the rain
It has many colors
Have you ever thought how it comes about?
It is said that the reflection of the light creates
different colors.
Is this a lesson, to teach us about others?
If the light can create different colors for us to see....
Then why is it so hard to see the beauty and
talents of others when asked what we like about
each other?

Stars

Stars are in the sky

They shine bright for all to see

But wait....who am I to be?

You can be whatever you can see...

Sitting inside

Today sitting inside is the way we are told to thrive
What if that is a mistake?
What to do if you need a break?
Go outside and see all the things around you that
live in nature
You may find a new reason to thrive, one that
you could not find inside

21

Birds

A bird always has a plan
No matter where it lands
It can always fly high in the sky

The Four Elements

The elements assist us in life
Air helps us breathe
Fire can keep us warm and can act as light in a
dark place
Earth provides us with lumber to build structures
to live and work in
Water helps plants grow and it keeps us alive, we
need it more than we realize
These are some examples of the importance of
the elements
Of nature in our lives as they help us thrive

The Joy of a pet

A pet is wonderful
Unlike people they do not judge
They give joy and love toys
They understand how you feel without words
Just by being present they have the power to heal

PEOPLE

A Friend

A friend is the opposite of a foe
A friend may keep you on your toes
Always wishing you well
Never letting you dwell on things that are not good for you
And you will do the same for your friend too

A Sister

A sister is a friend

She is there for you, whenever you need

You may not agree on some things

But together you can create wonderful memories

A Mother

A Mother is a person like no other
She puts others before herself
She helps keep the house in order
She cooks and cleans
However, you must remember she is also a person
With her own ideas and creativity
She is a person just like you and me

GOD/PRAYER/SOUL/ SPIRIT/ UNIVERSE

God

Some believe in God

Some do not

Whatever you choose is your own choice

Every person has his or her own voice

Just know a human makes mistakes

God/Spirit/the Divine provides a path for all

No matter how big or how small

Higher Power

When you feel you are alone
Know that we are all part of a divine plan
It is one not controlled by man although, he tries to
control what he thinks he can
If you have a moment in your life that feels like a tower
Know that there is a higher power
Guiding you to look ahead
It may be an unknown road
But you know you are never alone

Angel

An Angel is a divine being

A protector

One who is there to guide

At any time, always available

The key to contact this divine being is simple

Believe, *ask*, and *receive*

Prayer

Prayer can come in many forms
Some say it is a conversation with God/ Spirit/
the Divine
Others say it is a way to express gratitude for
what we have
Some pray for those who are ill
A person may pray to have strong will
Prayer is a way to express what you are feeling

My Soul

This life has a definite beginning and an end
Once our time is done that time is spent
It does not come back
However, the soul never ends no matter how
many lifetimes it spends
So, take time to nurture your soul
As uplifting your soul is the ultimate goal

The Universe

The Universe is *unlimited*

There is unlimited *abundance*

There is unlimited *love*

There is unlimited *potential* in the Universe

All you have to do is *see* it

Meditate

Take some time to be quite
Find a space
Where you can be alone
Without your phone
To help you get into the zone
Where you can see
Things that you were told could not be
The peace that you will find
After doing this for some time
Will blow your mind

Finding Light

The tools of prayer and meditation help create
peace within you
You will see how easy it is to find the light
Even in the darkest space there is a place for light
to shine
Just as the sun behind the moon lights up the
night sky

Balance

It is said that the universe exists in a delicate balance
Everyone has a yin and yang
When you are able to find this balance, there will
be an end to pain
You will have access to the talents you have within

Each of us is given a gift
It is up to you to see what it is
Once you find it
Develop it in order to share it with others

Numbers

The numbers one through nine are what we are

taught in school

They help us add and subtract

They help us tell time

But, what if numbers were a message from God/

Spirit/ the Divine?

Each number has its own meaning

Having a group of numbers together

May show what you want to know

In order to understand, you must be willing to

learn more than what you are told

Be bold, look for more and you will be sure to

find what you are looking for

Inner World

Look at me
I look inside *myself*
And find new wealth
For *within me* I find all that I can ever be
It is all *inside of me*

The Human Soul

Like every shoe, each person has a soul
In this life, each of us has a role
As you go through life, you will learn
That no matter where you turn
Your soul is with you guiding you towards *divine light*
The light that will brighten up your life

HOLIDAYS

Thanksgiving

A holiday in the fall
That reminds us all
Of all we are able to share
A chance to show that we care

Christmas Tree

My favorite tree

Is a *Christmas tree*

It is traditionally green

To me this creates a holiday scene

All the lights make the tree bright, and it acts as a

light in the dark of the night

It is a symbol that adds joy to the holiday season

My Own Valentine

I am my own valentine
I think it is fine
It is better to love yourself
Than to wait for some else

I love myself
For who I am
That is what matters
Instead of listening to others and their mindless chatter

Easter

A holiday in the spring
Where people get together
Hopefully to enjoy good weather
And express their gratitude to God/Spirit/the Divine
For this wonderful time, in which new plants shine

LESSONS

The New Alphabet

Creating a new alphabet

A – Always love life

B- Be real (and very entertaining)

C- Courage comes from within

D- Divine guidance comes from above

E- Everyday is a chance to learn something new

F- Friends help you

G- Great leaders listen

H- Have patience

I- If You believe it you can see it

J-Just be yourself

K- Kites are similar to ideas—run with them

L-love never dies

M – Me, myself, and I

N- Nothing can stop me

O-Open doors come to those who look for them

P- Perfection is not real

Q- Quite time is good for the soul

R- Reward yourself for small wins

S- See the good in things

T- The world is there for you to explore it

U- Uplift one person and you will feel good

V – Value the people around you

W- Why or why not is the question that should always be asked

X - Xray vision does not exist yet. See things as they are, not how you want them to be.

Y – you are unique

Z- Zebras have both black and white. They show us that there are at least two different ways of looking at one thing.

Finding New Meaning To Old Words

A lot of ideas are condensed into acronyms. I realized that some words can be acronyms that create a positive outlook on life.

Unstoppable
Now
Inspired
Quite
Unbreakable
Exquisite

Brave

Excellent

Amazing

Understanding

Trustworthy

Intelligent

Fun

Unbelievingly

Loving

Courage

Out

Now

For

Individual

Determination

Enlighten

Numerous

Certain to

Enrich

Gorgeous

Intelligent

Real

Loving

Powerful

On

Whatever

Endeavor

Realized

Stop and Ask Why

Today everything is rushed

Who knows why

We all try

To meet deadlines and make headlines

Even if that gives us nothing and makes us cry

Why do we try, if we don't know why?

What do you Value?

Some say money is most important
Others say it is the people around you
Yet someone else may say experience is the key
My question is do you listen to others?
Or do you say no, I listen to myself?
Do you know how to listen to your inner voice?
Or do you think you have no choice?
Whatever you choose, remember you decide
what to do.

Learning

Some say learning comes from books
Others say what you learn depends on who you know
Sometimes you learn from being hurt
The most important thing is that you keep learning
no matter what
Every person comes into your life for a different reason
It is up to you, how you see them

I Take Care of Myself

I create my own wealth

I have my health

I maintain good spirits

I know I am in charge of me

No matter what the problem of the day may be

Respect

Respect is something you should always have for yourself
You are a person with skills and talents
Who knows that respect is earned
Respect your body by giving it healthy food
Respect your mind by creating a happy mood

Know that others will respect you if you respect yourself
And that respect has nothing to do with material wealth
But with how you treat others and yourself

Feelings

Feelings can be strange
They can have a wide range
Some feelings can be very powerful
Know that feelings can help us realize what
emotional responses things in our lives create
But, be careful as feelings can make us want to
take actions that we may regret at a later date
Remember it is you who control how you feel
not others with whom you may deal
You choose how you feel

Emotions

Emotions can be described as energy in motion

Some are uplifting

Others help us see what is real

We know that energy is never lost

It takes a new form in order to help us learn

This life is about what we learn so that our souls

may return

In another time, more refined and closer to the

Divine

Always be You

Be You

It is important to be you

There is only one of you

That is why you must be true

True to your soul no matter what unfolds

It is important to be bold

Life is a gift

Life is a four-letter word
It contains the word "if"
This crucial the word in itself gives a clue
That you can do anything you want to....

As long as you *believe* you can....

The Power of Being a Girl

In countries outside the developed world, girls
are looked down upon
It is sad that it is so
Girls have so much potential to grow
Girls can give life, they can be someone's wife
They can teach or preach
If only they knew how much they could do
We may have a new outlook
That could change the way the world looks at
one of God's greatest creations
That help the world succeed in its never ending
need to change
Even though some still see a girl as girl just the same

The Power of a Lady

A lady is a human being
She has thoughts and feelings
She has a vision of what she wants to create
She works towards her goals without stopping
She knows that all is well
There is no time to dwell on what was in the past
As she is approaching her future fast
The present is where she lives
She gives but she knows that those who care will
give to her in return
So she knows that she is not alone
She has something that she can call her own

Listen

Sometimes there is too much noise
To try and find your voice
It is not easy
But if you are able to stay quiet
You may see what others cannot

Work of Art

A work of art can have a simple start
It does not matter how big or small
It comes as a call from within
It comes from the heart
That is what art is all about

Expression

People express thoughts and ideas in different ways
Some write, some draw, others create clothes
In whatever way you choose
Remember that there is no one
Who can fill your shoes
In the same exact way you do

Being able to express yourself may allow
You to create your own peace
No matter what challenges you meet
One by one pick up your feet
And see what an adventure you are on
And who you will meet
You may be surprised to see what you find over time

Time

What is time?

Is it something you can define?

Is it yours or is it mine?

All we know is that it is and that is fine

Mystery

There are things we call mysteries
What does this mean?
To me it means something that we do not know
There maybe those who do not want this
information to be known
May be they are part of our lost history
For example, we are told that we are descendants
of apes but maybe there is more
And in order to find it we must be willing to
explore and go where no one has ever gone before

Living or Existing

Some say you live life to the fullest
Others say you just exist
How do you know where you fit?
To know where you stand, ask what do I want to
do, stand by and let things happen, or do I want
to jump into action?

Educated

What makes you educated?

It is reading books?

Is it learning how to cook?

To me you define how you spend your time

It is up to you to decide what makes you gain

knowledge and for that you do not necessarily

have to go to college

Teaching

Everyone has the ability to teach
Everyone can teach different things
Why, you ask?
Because everyone has different gifts and talents
to improve human life in some way
What can **you** teach today?

A Home

A home is a place
Where you should feel safe
It should be your space
For you to create

Positive Self Talk

Are you happy with yourself?
If your answer is no, why?
What would you change?
To find the answers you have to take time to
think about what you want

And find a way to start looking at yourself in a
positive light
The positive light will guide you to fulfill your
potential to make your life bright

Thoughts Become Things

You have thoughts in your head
Your thoughts create your thinking
Your thinking creates a plan of action
Your plan of action creates things
This is why positive thinking is so important
If you think positive thoughts, you will create
positive things

Negative Thought

Negative thoughts are a reason for you to pause
It takes time to process thoughts that are not
pleasant like anger
But as you go through it
Know that you are not alone
This is the time to take rest, not to create a mess
Please know that this may take time
Please be kind to your mind
In the end you will be fine

The Morning

The first part of the day
At this time, you can get up and say *what a wonderful day*
You can decide what you need to do
Make a plan and know that you are able to
Create whatever is in your mind
Take things one step at a time
In this way you can say *I can make anything happen on any given day*

The Power of Vision

If you can think it
You can achieve it

Have a vision
As you work to create your vision
You may have a new position
In time you may find that creating a way for
others to assist you with your vision was in fact
your primary mission

Perception

Beauty is in the eye of the beholder
Some people look for physical attributes
Others see qualities that cannot be seen
The choice is yours to see what you wish
You *determine* what you consider *your own bliss*

The Power of Words

Have you ever thought about how what you say
affects others?
Sometimes you speak without thinking
What you say may affect different people in
different ways
Remember that what you say may have the
ability to make or break someone's day

Belief

A belief is something you are taught
Sometimes from others
Sometimes learned over time
Have you ever asked, is it really mine?

Fear

Fear may make you feel scared
What if it had a new meaning?

Forget
Everything
And
Run

False
Evidence
Appearing
Real

How do these new meanings make you feel?

Brave

To be brave you do not have to conquer a cave
You do not have to physically fight
You only need to know that it is good to help others
To care for those in need and sometimes let things be
That is what being brave means to me

Choice

Every person has choices in a day
Some will say there is too much to do
Take things slow and know that the choices you
make will take you to a place
If you do not like where you are
Make another choice and see if that helps
Remember that the things you do create
experiences for you
You will find what you like by making choices
Whether you think that they are wrong or right

Things do not Have to be Hard

Throughout life we learn many things
Some serve us, some do not
I have found one thing that has made me go
round and round

The idea that creating material wealth is hard
It is an idea that I now know is not true
And yet I still feel blue
A way of thinking that must be changed if I want
to be free
And I know that the change starts with me

Gratitude

It is said that an attitude of gratitude will lead the way

To a most glorious path each day

It may be hard to see sometimes

But know that as the days go on

You will notice little things

As you give your attention to these little things

You will feel that everyday feels like a win

And you will be grateful for where you have been

Inner Peace

This is something that is not talked about
Maybe because we are too busy trying to achieve
things that we think will bring it
However, I have learned that inner peace cannot
be bought or earned
It is something each of us create and it has no
expiration date

As Above so Below

If you want to create something new
Plant a seed and watch it grow
Who knows where you will go...

Work

Work is something you do
Some make it their whole life
Others believe work is only part of life
People choose what to do
Even if it is work that they do not truly want to
do
To me work should allow you to use your skills
and allow you to pay bills
Know that no matter what work you choose to
do, you are more than the work you do

Money

This is a five-letter word
That troubles people all over the world
Did you ever stop and think, why this one thing
causes so much pain?
It keeps so many people from doing what they
really love
It keeps parents working, while children are
alone at home

But, maybe we have the wrong idea about it
Maybe if we do what we truly love, it will rain
money from above

Stress

Stress is something everybody in life feels

It makes you reel

It creates a weird feeling

It also is a red flag that something may need healing

Think about with what you have been dealing

Take some time to create a peaceful state of mind

It is something you can do

To be in charge of you

Rest

What do you consider rest?

Do you take time to rest?

You should know that rest is as important as work

If you get proper rest, it is more likely that you

will perform at your best

Hurt

All humans have feelings
It is a fact that at some point you will get hurt
It is part of life, wrong or right
Know that every time you feel hurt, there is
something that will make you feel better

Space

Everyone needs space

People are able to work at their own pace

The space you are in may show where you have been

Space may allow you to clear doubts

Space is sometimes all you need to see that you are

ready to lead

Ideas

Some ideas come after beating your everyday drum
Some come when you hum
Others arrive when you are on a drive
It does not matter when or from where they come
What matters is what you do with them
The ideas you have may help solve a problem
They may help you through a difficult day
Either way it is you who has the idea and it is up to you
To decide to bring it into the light
The idea may help you thrive and feel alive

Colors

There are many colors
All colors symbolize different things
For example, green may represent growth
Yellow may represent the Sun or new beginnings
Blue may represent calmness
Purple may represent elegance
So, the next time you see a color, ask what does
this color mean to me?
You might surprised at what your answer may be

Embracing the New

Some people like to stick to what they know

That is good to have a flow

However, it is also important to grow

To do this you may go where no one has gone before

It is good to explore

Leader

A leader is a person
Who decides that helping others is more
important than thinking only of himself
Helping others learn something, guiding them to
something that may be new
A leader is one who decides that it is important
to have a voice in order to create a new choice

Freedom

Freedom means different things to different people
To me Freedom is being able to have your own thoughts
Freedom is being able to do what you want
When you want to do it
In the way that you want to do it
Freedom lets you be you

History

In my opinion, Winston Churchill was right
when he said "Those who do not know their
history are doomed to repeat it"[1].
To me it looks like we have to learn the lesson he
shared with us once again
It seems that we have also forgotten what Ronald
Regan said "Freedom is always one generation
away from extinction"[2].
If we all understood what these quotes meant, we
may not have been in this position today

---

1   *Winston Churchill Quotes*. (2019). Quote Tab. Retrieved February 15, 2022, from https://www.quotetab.com/quote/by-winston-churchill/those-that-fail-to-learn-from-history-are-doomed-to-repeat-it

2   *Ronald Regan Quotes*. (2021). Brainy Quotes. Retrieved February 15, 2022, from https://www.brainyquote.com/quotes/ronald_reagan_183965

Where the people we elected are ready, willing,
and able to take our freedoms away
This is why it has been said that it is important to
know history as they are lessons from those who
have come before us to teach us in the hope that
we will not repeat the same mistakes and make
the world a better place for all

We the People

Do you know your individual rights?
Do you remember why the farmers decided to fight?
Have you ever stopped to think
What would have been if they thought that they did
not have the power to protect their rights?
If asked to stand up for your rights today, what would
you say?

The Framers

The Framers were a small group
They were intelligent, hardworking, and motivated
Their goal was to govern themselves
They knew that had the ability to create a land of their own
A land that they could call home

The Flag

Red, White, and Blue

Stars and Stripes

All come together to create the symbol of our nation

This is a symbol that should be guarded and protected

And most of all respected

A Nation

A nation is created over time

The people are the creators of a nation

The people are given the gift of a nation

One which they should protect without hesitation

For if they do not stand to protect this gift

It may cease to exist

Voice

Each individual has a voice

Each one is capable of making his or her own choice

If you refuse to make a choice, you may look back

and say what if I had done something that day....

Organized

Just because something is organized does not
make it right
If it is organized one way that is one method of
doing something
You may see an alternative that is better that
takes less time
In the end all that matters is that you are able to
find a new way that may help someone one day
Even if it is not today

117

Sports

Sports are fun for some
Games are either lost or won
More important than the outcome
Is the fact that every player on the team has a role
Sports teach us to work together towards a
common goal regardless of the reward

Music

They say that food is fuel for the body and that
music is food for the soul
When people refer to songs written years before
they say old is gold
I think it is because songs written before had a goal

In Everyday Life

In this life we have been taught to turn off creativity
Instead, we sit in chairs and try to find reasons
To learn things that are not practical
Only later to find that we may have wasted time
Time is something we cannot get back
So why is it that we spend time doing things that do
not stimulate the mind?

What you Want

What you want may change over time
That is fine
When you are confused, you may want to take
some time to connect to the Divine
Remember that all of us are able to shine

Treat Yourself

The Golden Rule says Treat others the way YOU
want to be treated
The question is: How do *YOU* treat yourself?
Remember that if you are kind to others, you
should treat yourself with the same kindness

People

Know that everything in life happens for a reason
The same way that the year has different seasons
People are not all the same
Some look for others to blame
Some are willing to help you through pain
Those who assist you in improving yourself and
showing you they care
Are the ones you should keep for life, even if you
sometimes fight

Bonds

Bonds can be created through blood like families
They can be created through friendships
They can also be created through people you
meet and greet in your life
The bonds that you build and strengthen together
are the ones that will stand the test of time

Communicate

How do you communicate?

Do you talk to people in person?

Do you text?

Or do you send an e-mail?

What do you think suits you best?

Have you ever thought to try something new?

What do you think your kids will do?

The way we are going, there is no knowing

If people will have the desire to communicate at all

Will this be our biggest downfall?

Talk

Some say talk is cheap

Maybe that is why we tell stories to those we meet

The most important story of all is the one you tell
yourself

Think about that and see what you have said

What would you change?

All it takes is changing your story to unlock your own glory

Path of Life

Everyone in life follows a path

Some say the path of life is a straight line

That you follow over time

Others know that the path can change

At any given moment

The path may go in different directions

It may be a straight line or it may wind from time to time

The important thing is to keep going strong

On the path that you are on

Following this path is part of the journey that we call life

It may require all of your might

Know that from time to time you may have to fight for the

things you know are right

Without thinking about the reaction of others even if they

are people dear to you

You know what is right for you
Those who support you will see
The importance of what you need to be
So, remember that even if the road winds and bends
Everything will be alright in the end

Choosing Love for Myself

My dear how to you know who is true?

How do you know who to choose?

Do you know it is better to just choose yourself?

Why choose one if you know he is not good for you?

Choose yourself, put yourself first, and then see if he

chooses you

Trust

Trust is a key

It is very important to me

Why, well let's see

You are you and I am me

But in order to become a "we"

I have to trust you and you have to trust me

In order to create trust

Communication is a must

Our communication will show we are willing to

work together

To create something for you and for me

Trust is key

Eyes

The eyes are known as the window to the soul
They express how you feel
Your emotions are real
Find someone who appreciates your vision
Together create a world
That will be a secret to everyone but the two of you
And you will never question why things happen
the way they do
This is because you know that *the two of you made
your dreams come true*

Relationship

A relationship that is healthy involves two people
Each knows that they work together to help it grow
Each has his or her own life with work and friends
They come together to create something new
That they both want without losing themselves
Afterall, they like each other for who they are

Heart

The heart is a muscle in the body
It is strong, it keeps you alive
It is what allows you to thrive
If it breaks, mending it may take time
But know you will be fine

Love

Love is a feeling

It can be healing

It can grow with time

You can love anyone at anytime

Love is given to those we care for

Start by loving yourself and you will see all that

you can be

Happiness

Happiness is a key concept
Where does it come from?
Some say it comes from things you buy
Others say that it comes from those around you
For me, I know happiness comes from within
Happiness is something I create, I do not need to wait
I can create happiness, without having to wait for a
specific date

References

1. *Ronald Regan Quotes*. (2021). Brainy Quotes. Retrieved February 15, 2022, from https://www.brainyquote.com/quotes/ronald_reagan_183965

2. S.A.R.A.Y.U.T. (n.d.). © *Can Stock Photo / sarayut* [Loctus flower photograph]. CanStockPhoto. https://www.canstockphoto.com

3. *Winston Churchill Quotes*. (2019). Quote Tab. Retrieved February 15, 2022, from https://www.quotetab.com/quote/by-winston-churchill/those-that-fail-to-learn-from-history-are-doomed-to-repeat-it

About The Author

My name is Zafira Hudani. I am an attorney. I created this book by sharing with you the lessons I have learned in my life so far. I have gone through ups and downs like each of you. I have gone through the U.S. education system. I attended law school in England. I have a graduate degree in International Business Law. Throughout my education I have learned that your education does not necessarily come from sitting in class. The information that is given must be used in a way to create skills and help you question how to use/implement those skills.

I choose to look at the positive side of things. There are always good things that can come out of any situation you just have to find them. I hope this book gives you comfort and lets you know you are not alone in this journey of life.

Refer a Friend Page

Self-Publishing School

NOW IT'S YOUR TURN

Discover the EXACT 3-step blueprint you need to become a bestselling author in as little as 3 months.

Self-Publishing School helped me, and now I want them to help you with this FREE resource to begin outlining your book!

Even if you're busy, bad at writing, or don't know where to start, you CAN write a bestseller and build your best life.

With tools and experience across a variety of niches and professions,

Self-Publishing School is the only resource you need to take your book to the finish line!

DON'T WAIT

Say "YES" to becoming a bestseller:

https://self-publishingschool.com/friend/

Follow the steps on the page to get a FREE resource to get started on your book and unlock a discount to get started with Self-Publishing School

Next Steps/Working with me

If you would like to learn about my upcoming publications, please provide your e-mail address and I will send you an update with information about upcoming releases.

Link: **zafirahudanillc.com**

Review Ask Page

I would like to take this opportunity to THANK YOU for reading my book. THANK YOU for supporting me.

I would like to ask you to share your thoughts on my book. I look forward to writing more books that will connect with readers around the world.

Once Again, THANK YOU for taking the time to read my book. Your love and support is greatly appreciated.

Sincerely,
Zafira Hudani

Made in the USA
Columbia, SC
22 December 2022